I0796399

# Leo XIV
# The First American Pope

Bradley Steffens

San Diego, CA

Printed in the United States

**For more information, contact:**
ReferencePoint Press, Inc.
PO Box 27779
San Diego, CA 92198
www.ReferencePointPress.com



LIBRARY OF CONGRESS CATALOGING-IN-PUBLICATION DATA

Names: Steffens, Bradley, 1955- author
Title: Leo XIV : the first American pope / by Bradley Steffens.
Description: San Diego, CA : ReferencePoint Press, Inc, 2026. | Includes bibliographical references and index.
Identifiers: LCCN 2025032489 (print) | LCCN 2025032490 (ebook) | ISBN 9781678212582 library binding | ISBN 9781678212599 ebook
Subjects: LCSH: Leo XIV, Pope, 1955---Juvenile literature | Popes--Biography--Juvenile literature | LCGFT: Biographies
Classification: LCC BX1378.8 .S74 2026 (print) | LCC BX1378.8 (ebook) | DDC 282.092--dc23/eng/20250902
LC record available at https://lccn.loc.gov/2025032489
LC ebook record available at https://lccn.loc.gov/2025032490

# CONTENTS

# A New Leader for the Roman Catholic Church

When Pope Francis, the head of the Roman Catholic Church, died on April 21, 2025, his death set in motion a carefully choreographed process for selecting a new pontiff, or pope. Senior officials within the church, known as cardinals, gathered in Vatican City, a microstate located in Rome, Italy, that is the seat of the Catholic Church. On May 7, eleven days after the pope's funeral, 133 cardinals met in the historic Sistine Chapel to hold a special meeting, known as a conclave, to elect a new pope.

## An Unlikely Contender

According to church doctrine, any baptized Catholic man can become pope, but for centuries the cardinals have chosen someone from among their ranks to serve as the leader of the church. Nominating and voting within the conclave is secret, but Vatican insiders believed only a handful of cardinals were under consideration for the job. Among those mentioned was Cardinal Robert Prevost, an American and head of the pope's advisory group for naming new bishops.

Most Vatican observers discounted Prevost as a contender. The cardinals had never chosen a pope from the United States, and many believed they never would. Church leaders worried that selecting a pope from the world's preeminent political and economic power would concentrate too much authority in one country. Having a pope from a smaller, less powerful nation was seen as a way to counterbalance American influence.

## A Surprising Choice

The first three rounds of voting did not produce a consensus. In accordance with tradition, the ballots were burned in a way that produced black smoke rising from the chapel, a sign that no decision had been reached. Thousands of people waited outside for the signal of a decision. Millions more waited around the world to learn who would be the next leader of the 1.4 billion Catholics who make up the largest Christian denomination.

On May 8, 2025, white smoke rose from the Sistine Chapel, signaling the election of the 267th pope. About an hour later, Cardinal Dominique Mamberti, the most senior member of the College of Cardinals, stepped onto the Loggia of Blessings, a balcony overlooking St. Peter's Square. He spoke in Ecclesiastical Latin, the official language of the government headed by the pope, known as the Holy See. Mamberti said, "I announce to you a great joy: We have a pope." Mamberti then revealed the new pope's name: "The Most Eminent and Most Reverend Lord Robert Francis . . . Prevost, who has taken the name Leo XIV."[1]

> **"I announce to you a great joy: We have a pope."[1]**
>
> —Cardinal Dominique Mamberti, the most senior member of the College of Cardinals

Vatican watchers believe Prevost was seen by the cardinals as someone who could bridge the divide between progressives and traditionalists that had emerged during Pope Francis's mostly progressive papacy. Prevost's bishop advisory group had recommended both progressive and traditionalist candidates, showing an openness to all viewpoints. However, Prevost had not recommended radicals from either end of the spectrum, suggesting that he valued moderation.

Prevost seemed to have overcome the bias against choosing an American pope by virtue of the fact that he had served as a priest and bishop in Peru for twenty-four years. Prevost even became a

*Newly chosen Pope Leo XIV appears on the balcony of St. Peter's Basilica in Rome in August 2025.*

citizen of Peru in 2015 and continued to hold dual citizenship. In addition, from his years in Rome and Peru, Prevost had learned to speak Italian and Spanish as fluently as his native English. These factors led Vatican correspondent Iacopo Scaramuzzi of the influential Italian newspaper *La Repubblica* to call Prevost "the least American of the Americans."[2]

## Citizen of the World

As Mamberti withdrew into St. Peter's Basilica, officials unfurled from the balcony a large, maroon-and-white banner emblazoned with the emblem of the Holy See. A few minutes later, Pope Leo XIV stepped forward to greet the crowd and the world. He wore the traditional vestments of the pope—the mozzetta, a short red cape worn over the papal robe, and an embroidered stole. Pope Francis had declined to wear these outer garments for his first public appearance, hoping to convey an image of being close to the people. Pope Leo's donning of the vestments suggested that he would be more of a traditionalist than his predecessor.

With an attendant holding a microphone before him, Leo greeted the crowd in Italian. "Peace be with all of you," he said. A few moments later, the new pope mentioned Pope Francis, signaling a continuity with his predecessor that the progressives had hoped for: "Help us, one and all, to build bridges through dialogue and encounter, joining together as one people, always at peace. Thank you, Pope Francis!"[3] As he continued, Leo greeted Spanish speakers in the audience in their own language. He concluded his address with a blessing in Latin. Downplaying his connection to the United States, the pope did not say anything in English. Instead, he presented himself as a citizen of the world, a pope for Catholics everywhere.

**"Help us, one and all, to build bridges through dialogue and encounter, joining together as one people, always at peace."[3]**

—Pope Leo XIV

# Priestly Prodigy

Robert Francis Prevost was born on September 14, 1955, at Mercy Hospital, a Catholic hospital in Chicago, Illinois. His parents, Louis and Mildred Prevost, were devout Catholics. Their ancestors immigrated to the United States from several predominantly Catholic countries, including Italy, France, Spain, and the Dominican Republic. "I was born in the United States," Robert Prevost later said. "But my grandparents were all immigrants, French, Spanish. . . . I was raised in a very Catholic family."[4]

> "I was raised in a very Catholic family."[4]
>
> —Robert Prevost (Pope Leo XIV)

Robert's maternal grandfather, Joseph Norval Martínez, moved to New Orleans, Louisiana, from the Dominican Republic in the 1880s. Likely of mixed race, Martínez was listed in the 1900 US census as Black but in the 1910 census as White. In 1887 he married Louise Baquié at Our Lady of the Sacred Heart Catholic Church in New Orleans. Records indicate that Louise was a Louisiana Creole; that is, a member of a multiracial ethnic group in the former French and Spanish colonies of Louisiana. "It's clear that the Pope has centuries-long ties to free people of color in Louisiana,"[5] says professional genealogist Chris Smothers.

## A Heritage of Faith

Joseph Martínez worked as a cigar maker, a profession that requires a high degree of manual dexterity, concentration, and patience. While in New Orleans, the Martínezes had six daughters: Irma, Marguerite, Lydia, Louise, Hilda, and Ethel.

The family moved to Chicago sometime after 1910. There, they joined the parish of St. Mary of the Assumption Catholic Church. On December 30, 1911, the Martínezes had a seventh daughter, Mildred. Mildred was baptized on February 4, 1912, at Holy Name Cathedral in Chicago.

Mildred Martínez attended Immaculata High School, a private Catholic high school in Chicago. After graduation, she enrolled at DePaul University, a Catholic college in Chicago. She earned a bachelor of science degree in education in 1947 and a master's degree in education in 1949. Prevost's father, Louis Marius Prevost, also attended DePaul. A graduate of Central YMCA College, located in Hyde Park, Illinois, Louis was enrolled in the same graduate program as Mildred. He received his master of arts degree in education in 1948. After graduation, Louis became a teacher and Mildred a librarian. They married in 1949 and had three children: Louis Martín Prevost, John Joseph Prevost, and Robert Francis Prevost.

*Robert Francis Prevost (at left) is pictured with his mother and two brothers, Louis Martín and John Joseph.*

Louis and Mildred continued the Martínez family tradition of attending St. Mary of the Assumption Catholic Church. They were both parish lectors, laypeople who read from the scriptures during Mass. Mildred, or Millie, possessed a beautiful voice and sang in the church choir. She also helped start and build a library in the church's basement. "She was one of the ladies that we called church ladies," remembers Marianne Angarola, a former classmate of the future pope. "They went to Mass on a daily basis. They cleaned the altars, the church, the sacristy. She was involved in everything, including the fundraising activities."[6] Louis was more reserved, remembers former parishioner Betty Lyons-Geary. "He was always there for Millie. But he stayed in the background because she was always doing things at the parish."[7]

## Standout Student

The Prevost boys attended Mass with their parents and were enrolled in St. Mary of the Assumption School, a private Catholic school where the children all wore blue-and-white uniforms and attended Mass every morning. Robert was an excellent student. "[He was] the smartest person in the class," remembers former classmate Joseph Merigold. "Back in the day, they used to seat us by our classroom performance, so he always sat in the No. 1 seat, which was in the first row in the back."[8]

Robert was also noticeably devout. Former classmate Angarola remembers that he took his prayers seriously: "We used to pray with our hands, you know, our fingers pointing to heaven, and, after a while, you get tired of doing that, and you just want to fold them over. Robert Prevost never folded his hands over. He was just godly. Not in an in-your-face way. It was part of his aura, like he was hand-selected, and he embraced it. And he wasn't weird. He was nice."[9]

> **"Robert Prevost . . . was just godly. Not in an in-your-face way. It was part of his aura, like he was hand-selected, and he embraced it. And he wasn't weird. He was nice."[9]**
>
> —Marianne Angarola, former classmate of Robert Prevost

Robert's piety was not confined to the classroom. It was evident at home, as well. He used

## An Impressive Young Man

Dan King, a member of the board of education in Holland, Michigan, attended St. Augustine Seminary High School with Robert Prevost. Of the fifty students who started out in the freshman class, only ten—including King and Prevost—graduated. After Prevost became pope, King shared his thoughts about his former classmate:

> I remember some guys, they were two other kids in my class, they came running down the hallway and they said, “Dan, Dan, guess what?” And I said, “What?” “We just met somebody who’s smarter than you.” And I’m like, “Really?” And I went down to meet him. And I walked away from it saying, “I think he’s smarter than me.”. . .
>
> He was very humble, very, very humble, very quiet. But he was really nice, and I thought: “That guy’s going to go someplace.” . . .
>
> It’s just amazing that I . . . would have gone to school with a pope. You know, a normal guy, who grows up a normal kid just doing normal kid stuff, and he’s now in charge of what, 1.8 billion Catholics.
>
> I think he’s going to be a good guy for it. He’s the right guy.

Quoted in Josh Sanchez, “‘He’s the Right Guy,’ Says Holland Man Who Went to School with Pope,” Wood TV8, May 9, 2025. www.woodtv.com.

his outstanding memory and emerging talent for languages to re-enact the Catholic Mass, which at the time was said in Latin, the church’s official language. “You know how some kids like to play war, and be soldiers, and some girls want to play dolls, and be housewives?” says John Prevost, the pope’s older brother. “[Robert] wanted to play priest.” To set the scene, Robert would take out his mother’s ironing board and place a white tablecloth over it, creating a makeshift altar. He would then call his brothers and friends to his pretend service. “We went to Mass, and he knew everything,” John remembers. “He knew the prayers in Latin, he knew his prayers in English, and he did that all the time. . . . It was not a joke, it was not a game. He was dead serious about it.”[10]

## An Unusual Prediction

Even Robert’s neighbors noticed his devotion to the church. In a television interview shortly after his brother was named pope,

John recalled a strange prediction that not just one, but two neighbors made years earlier. "When [Robert] was in first grade, a woman across the street, whose kids we used to play with, and a woman down the street said that he would be the first American pope—in first grade they said that." When asked by the interviewer what he thought about the predictions, John replied, "We just laughed. He was six, so I was seven. Who knows what some lady is saying! But it stuck with me all this time. And then as he became a priest and then a bishop and then a cardinal, I thought, 'Maybe this is going to happen.' [Our parents thought] it

*Growing up, Prevost was a fan of the Chicago White Sox baseball team. Here, he is seen wearing a White Sox cap at the Vatican during a public appearance in 2025.*

was just children talking. Who's going to take something like that for real? . . . But someone saw something at that time."[11]

> "When [Robert] was in first grade, a woman across the street, whose kids we used to play with, and a woman down the street said that he would be the first American pope—in first grade they said that."[11]
>
> —John Prevost, brother of Robert Prevost

While religion was important to young Robert, he had other interests as well. "Growing up, we were just regular kids,"[12] says John. Like his brothers, Robert was a fan of the Chicago White Sox baseball team. Although generally well behaved in school, Robert was not perfect. "He was kind of a little trickster," remembers Merigold. "He used to poke me in the back of the head with a pencil all the time because I was a kidder. So he definitely had a sense of humor."[13]

As his Catholic education continued, Robert grew ever closer to the church. He became an altar boy, assisting the priest during the Mass by helping prepare the altar, carrying liturgical items like the cross and candles, and assisting with the preparation of sacred vessels used in sacraments such as baptism and communion. He also served as a lector, reading the scriptures aloud as part of the Mass.

## An Important Choice

When Robert graduated from St. Mary of the Assumption School at the end of eighth grade, he made a decision that would shape the rest of his life. Two of his mother's sisters, Louise and Hilda, had joined religious orders and become nuns. In line with the family's religious tradition, Robert asked his parents if he could attend a junior seminary, a school that would help prepare him for the priesthood. He had a specific school in mind: St. Augustine Seminary High School, a boarding school in Laketown Township, Michigan.

Robert's interest in St. Augustine Seminary High School did not have to do with its location but with its guiding philosophy. It was an Augustinian school. That is, it prepared students to join the Order of Saint Augustine, a community within the Catholic Church founded in 1244 by followers of Saint Augustine of Hippo. The order follows the fourth-century Rule of Saint Augustine, a credo

## Driving to Relax

Like many American teenagers, Robert Prevost got his driver's license while in high school. In college he enjoyed making the thirteen-hour, 700-mile (1,127 km) drive from Chicago to Villanova University in suburban Philadelphia. As a priest in Peru, he would often make the twelve-hour, 477-mile (768 km) drive from Chiclayo to Lima. Later, as the leader of the Augustinian Order, he enjoyed making the nine-hour, 572-mile (921 km) drive between Sydney and Brisbane, Australia. His older brother John says that the new pope has always loved to drive, and John expects that he will continue to drive as pope:

> We both learned to drive at the same time. He got behind the wheel and drove for a little bit. Then I got behind the wheel. . . .
>
> He loved to drive, just to go and drive to have a good time. That relaxed him—driving. . . .
>
> If he wants to drive around Rome, he's going to drive around Rome. He likes to drive. So I don't think he'll necessarily use a chauffeur.

Quoted in Maher Kawash et al., "Dolton Neighbor Told Young Cardinal Robert Prevost He Would Be Pope Someday, New Lenox Brother Says," ABC7 Chicago, May 8, 2025. https://abc7chicago.com.

emphasizing intellectual pursuit, community life, and pastoral service. The Augustinian Order is one of many communities within the Catholic Church, including the Dominicans, Franciscans, and Jesuits. Robert studied the various orders, and he felt drawn to the Augustinian intellectual tradition, which encourages deep reflection and has produced notable philosophers and theologians. He was also impressed with the order's reputation for fraternity. "As Augustinians, a core value for Augustine, is friendship," explains Reverend Robert Hagan, a member of the Augustinian Order. "We really can come to understand and meet the presence of God through friendship."[14]

Like traditional Catholic high schools, junior seminaries combine an academic curriculum—subjects like English, math, science, history, and foreign languages—with religious education, including the study of theology, sacred scripture, and church history. A major difference from traditional high schools is that seminarians receive spiritual guidance to help prepare them for priesthood. This pastoral care includes frequent opportunities for meditative prayer and confession. In addition, a junior seminary promotes a lifestyle that is different from the surrounding secular world. Located in the midst of hundreds of acres of woodlands along the shores of Lake Michigan, St. Augustine Seminary High School kept the students far from the distractions of ordinary life. This isolation helped foster a sense of purpose and community among the seminarians.

Like other junior seminaries, St. Augustine admitted only boys. The only times the seminarians interacted with members of the opposite sex was when they went home for Christmas and summer break. The separation from young women was intended to help the seminarians focus on their studies. It was also meant to prepare the young men for a life of celibacy.

*Prevost in his 1968 yearbook photo from St. Mary of the Assumption Parish, from which he graduated at the end of eighth grade.*

## Private Doubts

Prevost graduated from St. Augustine Seminary High School in 1973, a couple of months before his eighteenth birthday. He had originally planned to attend Tolentine College, an Augustinian seminary in Olympia Fields, Illinois, but it closed that year due to declining enrollment. He changed course and enrolled at Villanova University, near Philadelphia, Pennsylvania. Founded by the Order of Saint Augustine in 1842 and named after Saint Thomas of Villanova, Spain, Villanova University is one of only two Augustine institutions of higher education in the United States (the other being Merrimack College in Massachusetts). Along with other students who were planning to become priests, Prevost lived in a wing of a former Augustinian seminary that was converted into a residence hall. He majored in mathematics, but he continued to prepare for religious life by taking courses in Latin, Hebrew, and philosophy. He also continued reading the works of the early church writers and thinkers, especially Saint Augustine, and discussed theology informally with a circle of friends.

Unlike Prevost's high school, Villanova was a coeducational institution. For the first time in four years, Prevost was having daily contact with women his age. He began to wonder whether he was really cut out for a life of celibacy. On one of his visits home, he spoke to his father about his concerns. "Maybe it would be better I leave this life and get married; I want to have children, a normal life," Prevost said. His father replied that while the intimacy between a husband and wife was important, so was the intimacy between a priest and the love of God. That made sense to Prevost. He recalls thinking at the time, "There's something to listen to here."[15]

Prevost graduated from Villanova in 1977 with a bachelor's degree in mathematics. At this point, he faced a major decision. He could continue his studies in mathematics, which could lead to careers in teaching, business, or finance, or he could pursue his religious calling. He chose the priesthood.

# Answering the Call

From age fourteen, Prevost had been educated in Augustinian schools with the goal of joining the Order of Saint Augustine and becoming a priest ordained by a religious order. Not all Catholic priests are members of religious orders. In fact, most are not. About 80 percent of Catholic priests are diocesan priests, serving in geographic areas known as dioceses. Only about 20 percent are religious priests. Diocesan priests are not bound by the rule of a religious order, while religious priests are. Not everyone in a religious order is a priest, however. Some members of a religious order are lay members who are involved in various ministries or serve in the community. These lay members are known as brothers and sisters, or friars and nuns. Although they are not ordained, lay members take sacred vows, typically vows of poverty, obedience, and chastity. Even religious priests start out as lay members.

## Joining the Order of Saint Augustine

To begin his training as a priest, Prevost entered the Order of Saint Augustine in Saint Louis, Missouri, on September 1, 1977, thirteen days before his eighteenth birthday. He received his first training at the Augustinian Academy and the Immaculate Conception Church. The first year of training is known as the novitiate year, and the student, or candidate, is called a novice. As a novice, Prevost was given a white habit to wear as a symbol of his transition from his previous life to the life of the order.

*This school photo of Prevost is from 1977. That same year he entered the Order of Saint Augustine in Saint Louis, Missouri.*

Like other candidates joining the order, Prevost lived according to the values and mission of the Augustinians. He continuously reflected on his call to religious life, seeking guidance through prayer, spiritual direction, and community involvement. He participated in a full schedule of spiritual activities, including daily Mass, and the liturgy of the hours, a regimen that consists of seven daily prayers: morning prayer (lauds), daytime prayers (terce, sext, none), evening prayer (vespers), night prayer (compline), and the office of reading.

At the end of his novice year, on September 2, 1978, Prevost took his first vows of poverty, chastity, and obedience. These initial vows are also called simple, or temporary, vows. They are temporary because they must be renewed annually as candidates pursue their vocation. When candidates have completed their training, they take their final, or solemn, vows. His vows professed, Prevost traded in the white habit of a novice for the hooded black habit that Augustinian friars wear.

## Entering the Seminary

Prevost continued his preparation for the priesthood by enrolling at Catholic Theological Union (CTU) in Chicago, in the fall of 1978. Founded just ten years earlier and earning its accreditation in 1972, CTU is not just for Augustinians. It educates both diocesan priests and priests from several different religious orders. It also prepares laypeople for various ministries within the Catholic Church.

The school addresses not only academic development but also human, spiritual, and pastoral growth. Human growth is fostered by community living; spiritual growth is attained through continued attention to prayer and confession; and pastoral development is gained by working in various settings, including hospitals, prisons, and homeless shelters. Prevost worked with people who were addicted to drugs and alcohol. He could often be seen driving to hospitals and bars late at night to help people in need.

## Studying in Rome

Prevost received a master of divinity degree from CTU in 1981. He made his solemn vows on August 29, 1981, becoming a full-fledged Augustinian friar. Impressed with his scholastic record, his superiors sent him to Rome to study canon law—the laws that govern the church—at the Pontifical University of Saint Thomas

### Who Are the Augustinians?

The Order of Saint Augustine is a Catholic mendicant religious order. A mendicant order is one in which the members minister to a community, relying on charitable donations and their own work to support themselves, as opposed to monastic orders, where members live a more secluded life in a self-sufficient monastery.

The order was founded in 1244, when Pope Innocent IV united various hermit communities in Italy under the Rule of Saint Augustine, a short guide for religious life written by Augustine of Hippo in the fourth century. Augustine wrote some of the most important works of Christian theology, including *The City of God* and *Confessions*.

The order emphasizes community life, pastoral ministry, education, and the pursuit of truth, guided by the motto "One mind and one heart intent upon God." Augustinians live a life of interior reflection, communal harmony, and service to others. Their emblem—a flaming heart pierced by an arrow over an open book—symbolizes charity, divine inspiration, and the pursuit of knowledge.

The order currently includes about twenty-five hundred friars, of whom about eighteen hundred are priests, serving in nearly fifty countries. They operate parishes, schools, and missions and are active in theological scholarship and social outreach.

Order of Saint Augustine, "Who We Are," 2025. www.augustinianorder.org.

Aquinas. This was a turning point in Prevost's life. If he completed the program, he would receive a licentiate of canon law degree, an advanced degree that grants certain rights and obligations within the church. It would allow Prevost to teach canon law in a pontifical university or seminary and qualify him to join diocesan curiae, groups of officials who assist the diocesan bishop in governing a diocese. The licentiate degree is also a prerequisite for obtaining a doctor of canon law degree, a higher degree that would open up various positions in the church hierarchy.

The move to Italy helped Prevost in another way: It forced him to learn Italian. Arriving in Rome with a limited knowledge of Italian, he immersed himself in the language, studying it in the classroom, watching Italian television, and singing Italian folk songs. He soon became so fluent in the language that he was able to talk his way out of a jam when a police officer stopped him for driving the wrong way on a Roman street. His fluency in Italian would later help his career, since nearly half of Europe's cardinals are from Italy, and Italian is used for daily operations and administration in Vatican City.

*The Pontifical University of St. Thomas Aquinas in Rome, where Prevost studied canon law.*

In Rome, Prevost was ordained a priest on June 19, 1982, at the Augustinian College of Saint Monica. His parents, his brother John, and the two aunts who were nuns traveled to Rome for the ceremony that marked the fulfillment of his lifelong goal. Although it was not the last time the family would be together, it was the last time Robert's parents would see him elevated within the church. Mildred Prevost died in 1990 and Louis Prevost in 1997, in both cases long before their son was elevated to bishop, cardinal, and eventually pope.

Prevost stayed in Rome for the next two years, completing his studies in canon law. He received his licentiate in 1984 and began working on his doctoral dissertation, a long-form research essay that is required to complete a doctoral degree. He entitled his dissertation "The Role of the Local Prior in the Order of Saint Augustine." A local prior is the superior, or head, of an Augustinian community, such as a monastery, seminary, or college. The prior is responsible for the spiritual and material well-being of that specific community and for ensuring that it follows the Rule of Saint Augustine. Prevost acknowledged the need for a local prior to have strong local leadership skills. "In the end there must . . . be an individual who retains the authority to make decisions and to guide the life of the religious," Prevost writes. But he adds that the local prior is the servant of those he leads. "There is no room in Augustine's concept of authority for one who is self-seeking and in search of power over others. The exercise of authority in any Christian community requires the setting aside of all self-interest and a total dedication to the good of the community."[16]

> **"The exercise of authority in any Christian community requires the setting aside of all self-interest and a total dedication to the good of the community."[16]**
>
> —Robert Prevost (Pope Leo XIV)

## Missionary Work in Peru

In 1985, while working on his doctorate, Prevost was sent to Chulucanas, Peru, for his first missionary assignment. Again, he had to learn a new language quickly, and again it had an impact on his future career. Many of the cardinals who would vote for a new pope in 2025 came from Spain and the Spanish-speaking countries of North, Central, and South America. Prevost's eventual mastery of Spanish meant he was later able to communicate easily with one of the largest voting blocs among papal electors.

His first assignment in South America was to serve as chancellor of the Territorial Prelature of Chulucanas, an area in northern Peru. As chancellor, he maintained the church archives, including records of marriages, baptisms, and other sacraments. He also communicated important church information to the local clergy and parishioners.

He returned to Rome in 1987 to defend his doctoral dissertation in a public examination of the essay and the ideas closely related to it. He passed the oral exam and received his doctor of canon law degree that year. After defending his dissertation, he returned to the United States, where he served as vocation director and missions director of the Augustinian Province of Our Mother of Good Counsel in Chicago, Illinois. In this role he recruited members of the order for various missions.

Prevost was soon able to put his dissertation's ideas about the role of a local prior into action. In 1988 he was sent to Trujillo, Peru, to serve as the prior of an Augustinian seminary. As a local prior as well as the director of studies at the seminary, Prevost helped shape future priests, ensuring that they were prepared for both the theological and practical challenges of the priesthood. This was not merely an educational role. He traveled with the candidates as they served the local communities, building schools, improving health care services, and ministering to the poor. At the same time, he served as pastor at Our Lady Mother of the Church in a poor suburb of Trujillo. His approach emphasized living among the people, echoing the thoughts of Argentina's Cardinal Jorge Mario Bergoglio, the future Pope Francis, who called for priests to be "shepherds living with the smell of the sheep."[17]

*Prevost spent ten years in Peru. In this 2025 photo he meets a delegation from the Diocese of Chiclayo in Peru where he was bishop from 2015 to 2023.*

## Facing Danger

Peru at the time of Prevost's missionary service was a dangerous place. A Communist revolutionary group known as Shining Path was attempting to overthrow the government. The guerrilla warriors targeted the Catholic Church, which it saw as helping maintain the oppressive status quo. Members of Shining Path bombed churches and abducted and killed nuns and priests. Aware of the danger, church members often served as Prevost's bodyguards as he traveled from place to place.

To combat the Communist insurgents, the government forcibly recruited young men to fight in the army. One day a group of soldiers stopped a minibus carrying Prevost and his seminarians. The soldiers tried to remove the students from the vehicle and force them into military service. Knowing that a Peruvian law exempted members of the clergy from serving in the military, Prevost stood up to the soldiers' demands. "No," said Prevost, "these young men are going to be priests, they cannot go to the barracks."[18] Father Ramiro Castillo, one of the seminarians in the van that day, still marvels at Prevost's courage. "When he had to speak, he spoke,"[19] says Castillo.

Prevost also faced challenges in his role as a religious teacher. Many members of the South American clergy were proponents of liberation theology, a belief system founded by the Peruvian Dominican priest and theologian Gustavo Gutiérrez. Liberation theology emphasizes earthly liberation from social, political, and economic oppression, as opposed to the traditional Christian belief of enduring earthly existence in hopes of a better life after death. Prevost distanced himself from the more radical elements of liberation theology while embracing its core message of earthly justice and solidarity. He worked closely with the Latin American and Caribbean Episcopal Council, which had refined liberation theology into a theology of the people, focusing on grassroots pastoral care rather than political activism. "He had a deep grasp of Latin America's reality,"[20] observes Diego Garcia Sayan, a former justice minister in Peru.

**"When he had to speak, he spoke."[19]**

—Ramiro Castillo, reverend

After four years of serving as prior, Prevost was promoted to director of studies at San Carlos y San Marcelo, a diocesan seminary. In this role, he oversaw the academic aspects of the seminary, ensuring that the teachers were performing their du-

## Serving Those in Need

In 2017 Peru experienced severe flooding and mudslides due to the effects of El Niño, the climate pattern characterized by unusually warm ocean surface temperatures in the central and eastern tropical Pacific Ocean. Northern Peru, where Prevost was serving at the time, received ten times the normal amount of rainfall, causing rivers to overflow and triggering landslides. Prevost joined with members of his diocese to provide relief to the people hardest hit by the floods. Mariana Quiróz, who worked beside Prevost, remembered him wading through the high waters to help out. "He wasn't a man of the desk, but a man who worked with the people," says Quiróz. "People were suffering so much. Many were left homeless. And the father was there."

Quoted in Mitra Taj et al., "In Chiclayo, Peru, Locals Cheer the 'Peruvian Pope,'" *New York Times*, May 9, 2025. www.nytimes.com.

ties and that students were progressing academically. At the same time, he continued to serve as pastor of Our Lady Mother of the Church.

> **"He had a deep grasp of Latin America's reality."[20]**
>
> —Diego Garcia Sayan, former Peruvian justice minister

After his mother died in 1990, his father decided to visit him in Peru. Louis Prevost spent time observing his son as a priest, professor of canon law, and school administrator. A retired school administrator himself, Louis was impressed with what he saw. "He was so proud of his son,"[21] remembers Bishop Daniel Turley, who lived there at the time.

The ten years Prevost spent in Peru provided him with important pastoral experience and a deep understanding of Latin American Catholic life. This period confirmed many of the ideas he had written about in his dissertation, especially the need for a prior to serve his community and to listen to its members, rather than issuing top-down orders. Without his knowing it, this period was quietly preparing him for future roles within the church.

# Rise to Bishop

John Prevost says that his younger brother enjoyed his work in Peru. "I think in his heart, if he had his druthers, he would still be there. He liked missionary work. He liked working with the poor. He liked working with the disadvantaged."[22]

> "I think in his heart, if he had his druthers, he would still be [in Peru]. He liked missionary work. He liked working with the poor. He liked working with the disadvantaged."[22]
>
> —John Prevost, brother of Robert Prevost

However, in 1998 the provincial council in Chicago elected Prevost to lead the Augustinian Province of Our Mother of Good Counsel as its provincial prior. His election required the forty-three-year-old priest to leave the community he had come to love and return to Chicago. He began serving in his new position in March 1999. Although Prevost missed the parishioners, students, and friends he had made in Peru, his election to provincial prior raised his profile within the Augustinian order worldwide.

## Heading the Global Order

After serving two years as provincial prior, Prevost traveled to Rome in September 2001 for the 180th meeting of the General Chapter of the Augustinian Order. This is a gathering of representatives from various parts of the order, including provinces, vicariates, and local communities. The General Chapter is the highest decision-making body of the order. It meets every six years to address matters of governance, ministry, and the overall well-being of the order. The General Chapter also chooses the prior general, the global head of the Augustinian order and its supreme authority. Although Prevost had been a provincial prior for only two years, the General Chapter elected him to be the global leader of the Augustinian Order.

Considering his brief term as provincial prior, Prevost was a surprising choice for prior general. In this case, his youthfulness worked for him. The organization wanted a man with energy and passion who could cope with the demands of the office. In addition, Prevost's degree in mathematics revealed a facility with numbers that would help in areas like budgeting, auditing, and fundraising. His mastery of languages—English, Spanish, Italian, and Latin—was also seen as a plus, enabling him to communicate comfortably with provincial priors and members around the world.

At the time of Prevost's election as prior general, John Paul II was pope. Although the pope could not attend the General Chapter in person, he addressed it via video. He encouraged the order to reflect on its past and look forward to its future:

> I welcome you with joy, on the occasion of your General Chapter. I especially greet the Prior General and thank him for having expressed the kind sentiments of all present. . . . Your most important task is to preserve, unaltered and living, the heritage and the message of the life and doctrine of St Augustine, in which humanity in its quest for truth, happiness and love in every age can recognize itself. . . . I repeat to you what some years ago I wrote to all consecrated persons: "You have not only a glorious history to remember and to recount, but also a great history still to be accomplished!"[23]

## Building Relationships Around the World

Inspired by the pope's words and energized by the challenge of overseeing a global organization, Prevost worked tirelessly in his new position. He returned to Vatican City, where the Augustinian Order is headquartered. Reelected to the position in 2007, Prevost ended up spending twelve years in Rome, raising his profile even more among Vatican officials. He also formed new relationships as he traveled around the world, meeting with provincial priors and their communities on every continent except Antarctica.

It was on one of these trips that Prevost met Cardinal Bergoglio, the future Pope Francis, in Argentina. The two men had a lot in common, including their service in South America, a leadership style that involved listening to the community, and a moderate view of liberation theology. But they also had differences. "I'm not going to tell you the reason, but let's just say that not all of my encounters with Cardinal Bergoglio ended in agreement,"[24] Prevost later told his fellow Augustinians.

In 2013, Pope John Paul II's successor, Pope Benedict XVI, resigned from the papacy, and Cardinal Bergoglio was elected pope, taking the name Pope Francis. A few months later, Prevost invited Francis to lead the Mass at the 182nd General Chapter, something that popes rarely do. To Prevost's surprise, the pope agreed. At the Mass, Prevost called the pope "a great gift"[25] to the Catholic Church. Afterward, Francis told Prevost, whose

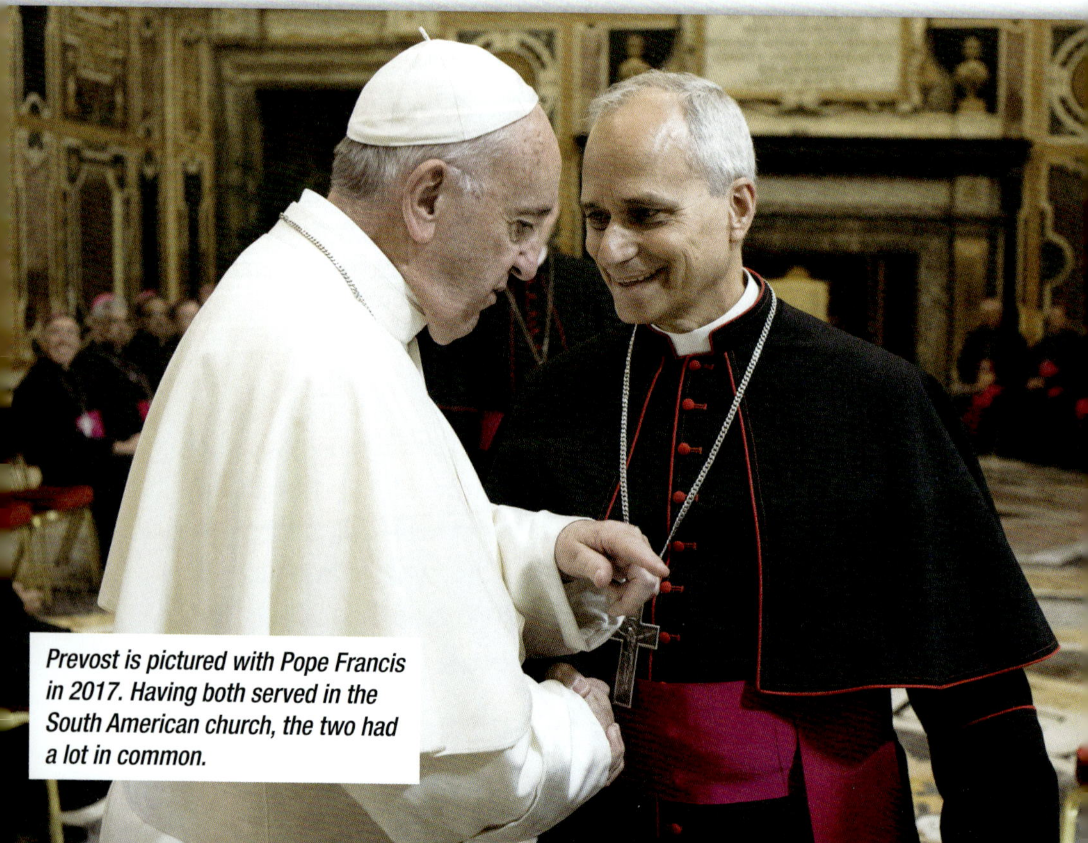

***Prevost is pictured with Pope Francis in 2017. Having both served in the South American church, the two had a lot in common.***

## The Importance of Reflection and Meditation

Every six years representatives of the Augustinian Order meet to discuss matters of importance to the order and to choose its leader for the next six years. In 2001, when the representatives chose Robert Prevost to head the order, Pope John Paul II addressed the group. In his speech, the pope talked about Saint Augustine's teachings about the importance of self-reflection and meditation:

> Augustine's experience is similar to that of many people today. For this reason, Augustinian Fathers, with modern forms of pastoral service, you can help them to discover the transcendent meaning of life. . . .
>
> You, dear Augustinian fathers, are the "teachers of interiority" at the service of people of the third millennium. . . . It is always Augustine who reminds us that only drawing close to one's own interior center of gravity makes possible contact with the Truth that reigns in the spirit.
>
> To succeed in reaching this haven, starting point and goal, as St. Augustine noted in the *Confessions*, a work of immersion in ourselves is necessary, of freedom from being conditioned by the exterior world, of attentive and humble listening to the voice of conscience.

Pope John Paul II, "Address of John Paul II to the Members of the 180th General Chapter of the Order of St. Augustine (OSA)," Holy See, September 7, 2001. www.vatican.va.

term as prior general had come to an end, to rest up, suggesting he might have another assignment for him.

His terms as prior general completed, Prevost returned to the Province of Our Mother of Good Counsel in Chicago. There, he took on dual roles, as he had in Peru. One of his jobs was to serve as director of formation at the Convent of St. Augustine in Chicago, a friary where men in the Augustinian Order complete their theological studies and live after professing their first vows. The director of formation oversees the education, training, and spiritual development of the friars as they progress toward their solemn vows. Prevost's other job was to serve as first councilor and provincial vicar of the Province of Our Mother of Good Counsel. The provincial vicar is the second-highest office in the province, just under the provincial prior. The provincial vicar acts as a substitute for the provincial prior in his absence, whether due to illness, travel, or other circumstances. The rest of the time, the provincial vicar helps the provincial prior ensure that the province is functioning well. This includes offering guidance and leadership to the friars and communities, serving as a point of contact for the province, and communicating with various groups and individuals, including other religious orders and the public. Having already served as provincial prior of the Province of Our Mother of Good Counsel and as prior general for the global Order of Saint Augustine, Prevost was overqualified for this position, but he was happy to step out of the limelight and serve the order in whatever capacity was needed.

## Elevation to Bishop

The situation did not last long. In 2014, Pope Francis sent Prevost back to Peru, appointing him apostolic administrator of Chiclayo, the capital of Chiclayo Province in northern Peru. An apostolic administrator in the Catholic Church is a priest appointed by the pope to oversee a diocese that does not have a bishop. Apostolic administrators are equivalent in canon law with diocesan bishops, meaning they have essentially the same authority as a diocesan bishop.

Prevost faced several challenges when he arrived in Chiclayo. First, the diocese was in financial disarray due to scandals involving financial mismanagement. Here, Prevost drew on his degree in mathematics and his twelve years of experience as prior general to assess the extent of the mismanagement. He then made and enacted a plan to return the diocese to financial stability.

Another challenge in Chiclayo was one he had faced before during his ten years as prior in Trujillo; namely, the growing tensions between liberation theology and traditional Catholic doctrine. As before, he launched social outreach programs, education initiatives, and economic empowerment efforts to make the church a voice for the marginalized without becoming entangled in partisan politics. At the same time, he upheld traditional Catholic teachings, particularly in areas such as clerical discipline, liturgical practice, and doctrinal integrity. He faced criticism from both progressive and conservative factions. Some accused him

In 2014, Prevost went back to Peru and became apostolic administrator of Chiclayo. The Chiclayo main square and cathedral are pictured here.

of being too cautious in addressing social injustices, while others feared he was too open to reform. His ability to navigate these tensions with diplomacy and pastoral sensitivity earned him respect within the Vatican. Recognizing his effectiveness, Francis formally named Prevost Bishop of Chiclayo in 2015.

## Dealing with Scandal

As bishop, Prevost focused on strengthening seminary education, continuing to improve the diocesan financial governance, and advocating for social justice. On the surface, everything seemed to be going well. But several years into his term as bishop, Prevost learned that three nuns had accused two priests from his diocese of sexual abuse. Afraid that a scandal might jeopardize their ability to become nuns, the young women kept silent until they had taken their solemn vows. In April 2022 the nuns came forward with their accusations.

According to a 2023 report by the Office of Social Communications of the Diocese of Chiclayo, Prevost personally met with the victims. After hearing their story, he opened an initial church investigation. He also encouraged the victims to take their story to the "listening center" he had recently created for handling

## Practicing What He Preached

As prior general, Prevost traveled the world. Wherever he went, he promoted inculturation, the practice of respecting local traditions and indigenous communities and taking care to have Catholic teachings resonate with them. To demonstrate his openness to other cultures, Prevost would visit local landmarks, wear local clothing, and sample the local cuisine. In Nigeria, he donned flowing robes and a cap. According to Rev. Luciano DeMichieli, who traveled with Prevost, the prior general was "not picky" about food and was willing to try anything. In the Philippines, he gamely ate *balut*—hard-boiled fertilized duck egg. Prevost later said it took him three days to digest the Filipino delicacy.

Quoted in Jason Horowitz et al., "Long Drives and Short Homilies: How Father Bob Became Pope Leo," *New York Times*, May 17, 2025. www.nytimes.com.

abuse complaints. The listening center was overseen by a commission composed of priests, a lawyer, and four psychologists. Prevost also encouraged the nuns to bring their accusations to law enforcement officials so the priests could be investigated and brought to justice under the law. Prevost immediately suspended one of the priests from the ministry, pending the completion of the investigation. At the time the young women came forward, the other priest was no longer in the ministry due to his age and health. As a result, Prevost took no action regarding him.

In July 2022 Prevost sent the results of the church's investigation to the Dicastery for the Doctrine of the Faith (DDF) in Rome for review. The DDF is the Vatican office that oversees such complaints. Local law enforcement refused to investigate the charges because the statute of limitations had expired. In addition, the DDF closed the case because, in the words of the report by the Diocese of Chiclayo, "the accusations brought against the accused priest have not been sufficiently proven."[26] The nuns went public, claiming that Prevost failed to properly investigate the accusations. The Vatican determined that Prevost had followed the proper procedures and done everything that was required by church law. Pedro Salinas, a Peruvian journalist who investigates sexual abuse cases involving the clergy, stated that the allegations against Prevost were not true. "There is no documentary evidence or solid testimonies pointing to Prevost,"[27] Salinas said.

## Environmental Issues

Prevost also faced criticism for his response to environmental justice. The Catholic Church has supported environmental justice for decades. In his 1990 World Day of Peace message, Pope John Paul II said "the ecological crisis is a moral issue"[28] and warned against the burning of fossil fuels. John Paul II's successor, Benedict XVI, taught that cultivating peace begins with protecting creation, and he warned against indifference toward the environment. Pope Francis went even further in 2015, issuing a 180-page encyclical titled *Encyclical Letter Laudato Si' of the Holy Father Francis on Care for Our Common Home*. An encyclical is an official letter from the pope to the bishops of the Roman Catholic Church on matters of church doctrine, morals, or social issues. In *Laudato Si'*, as the encyclical came to be known, Francis stated that climate change is a pressing global issue that requires action. "There is an urgent need to develop policies so that, in the next few years, the emission of carbon dioxide and other highly polluting gases can be drastically reduced,"[29] he wrote. In 2018 some Peruvian environmental advocates expressed disappointment that Prevost did not

> **"The ecological crisis is a moral issue."[28]**
>
> —Pope John Paul II

*Pope Francis was outspoken about the environment. This photo shows a 2023 handout for a press conference on Pope Francis's sencyclical letter on environment,* Laudato Si'.

always take a public stand on local environmental issues, including mining pollution, deforestation, and land disputes.

Although not as bold as Francis, Prevost did speak out on the environment. Prior to the 2015 United Nations climate summit in Paris, Prevost took to Twitter (now X) and posted a photograph of people carrying a banner picturing Francis and referring to *Laudato Si'* at a climate march in Chiclayo. Prevost wrote on the post, "The planet needs us."[30] Prevost linked another of his posts to a petition organized by the Global Catholic Climate Movement to collect 1 million Catholic signatures in support of a global climate agreement. Above the link he wrote in all capital letters, "SIGN THE CLIMATE PETITION."[31] The ensuing climate agreement, known as the Paris Agreement, was signed by 195 entities, including the United States. Two years later, newly inaugurated President Donald Trump issued an executive order to weaken emissions limits on power plants and roll back international climate change financing. In response, Prevost retweeted a story about the Catholic Relief Services, an international development agency, expressing concern that the United States would not meet its carbon emissions target under the Paris Agreement. When Trump announced his intention to withdraw from the agreement altogether, Prevost retweeted a post urging the president to read *Laudato Si'*, a copy of which Francis had sent to Trump. On Earth Day 2019, Prevost retweeted a Peruvian Episcopal Conference post with an illustration of Francis hand in hand with indigenous people and the message "Let us take care of our Mother Earth, just as different cultures have done throughout history and as they do today."[32]

**"The planet needs us."[30]**

—Robert Prevost (Pope Leo XIV)

Despite the criticisms and controversies that arose during his tenure as bishop, Prevost was recognized by Francis for his administrative competence, particularly in modernizing diocesan finances and improving seminary training. His leadership style—firm yet compassionate, traditional yet open to dialogue—made him a natural candidate for higher responsibilities within the Vatican.

# Vatican Leadership

Prevost's steady handling of his diocese, his experience as prior general of the order, and his relationship with Pope Francis dating back to the pope's days as a cardinal in Argentina, put Prevost on a fast track within the Catholic Church. From 2019 to 2024, Francis promoted Prevost six times, raising him higher and higher within the church's hierarchy.

In July 2019, Francis appointed Prevost to the Congregation for the Clergy, now known as the Dicastery for the Clergy. The dicastery is a department within the Roman Curia, the central body that assists the pope in governing the Catholic Church. Members of the Dicastery of the Clergy oversee diocesan priests and deacons in the same way that provincial priors oversee religious order priests and friars. Both offices supervise the training and ongoing formation of priests. The officials also handle matters related to the priests' pastoral ministry. With his experience as a provincial prior for the Augustinians, Prevost was an obvious choice for the dicastery.

The next year, in November 2020, Francis promoted Prevost to the Congregation for Bishops, later renamed the Dicastery for Bishops. Another department within the Roman Curia, the Dicastery for Bishops identifies and recommends candidates to the pope for consecration as bishops. While the pope is free to make anyone he wants a bishop, in most cases he accepts the choices presented to him by the dicastery. In addition to this human resources function, the Dicastery for Bishops is also involved in the creation of

*Members of the Dicastery for Bishops attend regional or national conferences of bishops to address regional issues. This photo shows a 2021 bishops' conference at the Vatican.*

new dioceses and the reorganization of existing ones. The church believes it is important for bishops to meet with the pope and other Vatican officials, and the dicastery is responsible for arranging such visits. The dicastery's members also reach out to bishops around the world, attending regional or national conferences of bishops to address regional issues. With his managerial skills, his fluency in English and Spanish, and his knowledge of the Catholic communities in North and South America, Prevost was highly qualified to serve in the dicastery.

## Called Back to Rome

In January 2023, just over two years after Prevost became a member of the Dicastery for Bishops, Cardinal Marc Ouellet—the prefect, or head, of the dicastery—resigned. The Vatican announced that Francis accepted Ouellet's resignation because of the prefect's age. At seventy-eight years old, Ouellet, a Canadian cardinal, was three years past the traditional clergy retirement age of seventy-five. However, Ouellet had also recently been accused of sexual misconduct by two adult women. Ouellet was also named

> **"If I name Prevost as the head of the office for the bishops, how do you think he will do?"[34]**
>
> —Pope Francis

in a class action lawsuit against the Archdiocese of Quebec, in which 101 alleged victims accused eighty-eight clerics of sexual abuse dating back decades. Ouellet denied all of the allegations and filed a countersuit against the woman who accused him of sexual assault, seeking $100,000 in damages for "injury to his reputation, honor and dignity."[33] Nevertheless, he stepped down.

Francis wanted to fill the vacancy with Prevost, but he was not sure how the bishop would be accepted by the more senior clergy. The dicastery is mostly made up of cardinals and archbishops, with a smaller number of bishops, of which Prevost was one. Francis summoned Father Moral Antón, the man who had succeeded Prevost as the prior general of the Order of Saint Augustine, to discuss the matter. "If I name Prevost as the head of the office for the bishops, how do you think he will do?" Francis asked Antón. The prior general said he thought Prevost would do well. "I also think he will,"[34] Francis replied.

The pope then met with Prevost and told him that he was considering him for the high office. "Whether you decide to appoint me or to leave me where I am, I will be happy; but if you ask me to take

## Prevost's Message on Climate Change

Like other nations, the Holy See hosts embassies from many countries. In November 2024 the Holy See embassies of Cuba, Bolivia, and Venezuela held a seminar on climate change entitled "Addressing the Problems of the Environmental Crisis in Light of *Laudato Si'*," referring to Pope Francis's encyclical on the environment. In his role as president of the Pontifical Commission for Latin America, Prevost addressed the seminar. He said it was time for governments, industry, and individuals to move "from words to action." Such action, he continued, should be in line with the social doctrine of the Catholic Church as set forth in the papal encyclicals on climate change and its impact on the poor and indigenous peoples. Prevost condemned the notion that human beings have unrestrained authority over nature. "Dominion over nature—the task which God gave humanity—should not become tyrannical," Prevost said. "It must be a relationship of reciprocity with the environment."

Quoted in Kielce Gussie, "Pope: Climate Change Impacts Poorest and Requires Global Cooperation," Catholic News Service, November 29, 2024. www.vaticannews.va.

> "Whether you decide to appoint me or to leave me where I am, I will be happy; but if you ask me to take on a new role in the Church, I will accept."[35]
>
> —Robert Prevost (Pope Leo XIV)

on a new role in the Church, I will accept,"[35] said Prevost. On January 30, 2023, Francis named Prevost prefect of the Dicastery for Bishops. The prestigious appointment required Prevost to return to Rome.

At the time Ouellet resigned, he was also serving as president of the Pontifical Commission for Latin America. The purpose of the commission is to study the church in Latin America, which is home to nearly 40 percent of the world's Catholics. Once again Prevost's fluency in Spanish and his decades of experience in Latin America served him well. The pope appointed him to head the commission. In honor of his promotions and to allow Prevost to keep his hand in the Peruvian church, Francis gave Prevost the title of archbishop-bishop emeritus of Chiclayo.

As prefect, Prevost made sure that the dicastery recommended candidates for bishop who would be aligned with Francis's emphasis on humility, service, and inclusivity. In particular, Prevost wanted to be sure that future bishops were committed to Francis's synodal vision. Synodality emphasizes a shift from a top-down hierarchical structure to a more bottom-up, participatory model of governance and decision-making. This means that the voices and perspectives of the local communities and ordinary members are valued and integrated into the church's life and mission, rather than solely being directed from the top. However, Prevost interpreted synodality cautiously, stressing that it must operate within the church's doctrinal framework. As a result, his selections for bishop leaned toward centrist figures, avoiding both hard-line traditionalists and reformists. Reformist scholars like Massimo Faggioli argued that Prevost's approach risked synodality without real change, while many traditionalists distrusted his openness to dialogue.

One of Prevost's most noteworthy responsibilities was overseeing Francis's historic reform of allowing three women to participate in the selection of bishops—a groundbreaking move that signaled greater inclusion for women in church governance. This decision was met with mixed reactions, with progressives celebrating it as a step toward equality, while conservatives viewed it as a departure from tradition.

## Elevation to Cardinal

Pleased with Prevost's leadership of the dicastery, Francis elevated him to the position of cardinal in September 2023. Cardinals are the highest-ranking members of the Catholic clergy, second only to the pope. However, there are three ranks of cardinals. The highest rank is cardinal bishop. Only six cardinals hold this title. Each one holds jurisdiction over a church in a suburb of Rome while working in the Roman Curia. The second-highest rank is cardinal priest. Most cardinals are cardinal priests. They serve in dioceses outside Rome. For example, all of the cardinals in the United States are cardinal priests. The lowest level is cardinal deacon. Cardinal deacons include officials of the Roman Curia. Once elevated to cardinal, cardinal deacons are assigned to a church in one of three deaconries, or diaconates, of Rome. This is the position Francis gave Prevost, assigning him to the Diaconate of

*Pope Francis is pictured here at the Venice Biennale, looking at art that included works by female inmates of a Venice prison.*

Saint Monica, a church near the Vatican that is associated with the Augustinians. Prevost officially took charge of this church in January 2024.

Believing that Prevost brought insight and good judgment to his role as precept of the Dicastery for Bishops, Francis wanted to involve the new cardinal in as many areas of church governance as he could. In October 2023, Francis appointed Prevost as a member of seven more dicasteries. The flurry of appointments left no doubt that Francis viewed Prevost as an important voice within the church, possibly even a suitable successor.

As head of the Dicastery of Bishops, Prevost accompanied the pope on his Apostolic Journeys, visits to a specific location for the purpose of fulfilling religious duties and strengthening ties with local communities. All of these visits were to events held in Italy in 2024. In April the pope attended the Venice Biennale, an international art exhibition that included works by female inmates of a Venice prison. In May he traveled to Verona to chair an event focused on promoting peace and justice by holding discussions on social issues. In June, Francis attended the 50th G7 Summit in Fasano, a meeting where the heads of state from seven major

## A Prayer for Pope Francis

On the evening of March 3, 2025, twilight descended over St. Peter's Square as hundreds of the faithful gathered to lift their voices in prayer for the health of Pope Francis. On the steps of St. Peter's Basilica, Cardinal Prevost led the rosary with a solemnity that touched pilgrims and prelates alike. As candles flickered and the beads of the rosary passed reverently through prayerful hands, Prevost's invocation echoed through the square: "Let us pray with Mary, Mother of the Church, for the health of the Holy Father Francis. She, Mother of Holy Hope, comes to assist and console all who call upon her. Be also for us this evening a sign of consolation, of sure hope in God. O God, draw near to us—let us find rest together in You."

Less than two months later, on the evening of April 21, 2025, Cardinal Mauro Gambetti, archpriest of St. Peter's Basilica, led another recitation of the rosary for Pope Francis on the basilica steps. This time, it was to give thanks for the life of the pope, who had died that morning.

Quoted in Vatican News, *March 3 2025, Holy Rosary Presided Over by H.E. Cardinal Robert Francis Prevost*, YouTube, March 3, 2025. https://youtu.be/LOwWqbviR8I?si=3D8LC2XLUSHq3UdY&t=165.

Pope Francis on the "popemobile," makes his last tour to greet the faithful in St. Peter's square, on Easter Sunday, 2025.

industrial countries discuss global policy issues. In July, Francis visited Trieste in 2024 to participate in the 50th Italian Catholic Social Week, an annual gathering focused on Catholic social doctrine and its application to contemporary issues. In October the pope attended the 16th Ordinary General Assembly of the Synod of Bishops in Rome, a monthlong conference designed to promote a greater emphasis on synodality in the church.

On all of these pastoral visits, Prevost assisted and advised the pope. He also saw firsthand how a pope conducts himself in public and interacts with people from all walks of life—world leaders, church officials, artists, activists, students, and prisoners.

## Promotion to Cardinal Bishop

In early February 2025, Francis began to experience breathing difficulties. On February 5 the pope appeared at the weekly general audience at the Vatican as usual and greeted the crowd. Smiling but pale, the pope added, "I must ask for your pardon. Today, because of this strong cold that I have, I ask for my collaborator to read this catechesis [teaching]. I am sure that he can read it better than I can in this moment."[36] The next day the Vatican press office announced that the pope was suffering from bronchitis. In the grips of the illness, Francis elevated Prevost to cardinal bishop, the highest rank within the church after the pope.

Three days later, on February 9, the still ailing pope presided over the Mass for the Jubilee of the Armed Forces, the second major event of the Holy Year of Hope—a year marking the 2025th anniversary of the birth of Jesus Christ. The pope was too ill to say the liturgy, recite the prayers, or administer the sacraments, so he had Prevost do it instead. Five days later, Francis was admitted to Gemelli Hospital in Rome. His condition worsened. On February 18 the Vatican announced that the pope had bilateral pneumonia, indicating that he had an infection in both lungs. On March 3 the pope suffered two episodes of acute respiratory failure, the Vatican's press office said. That day Prevost presided over a praying of the rosary for Francis's health in St. Peter's Square.

The pope was discharged from the hospital on March 23 but remained in delicate condition. On April 19, Francis made a short, unannounced visit to St. Peter's Basilica to pray before the Saturday evening Easter vigil. The next day, Easter Sunday, the pope appeared in St. Peter's Square for an Easter blessing. To the surprise of the thousands assembled in the square, the pope took a ride in the open-air "popemobile" to greet the crowds. That night, Francis thanked his personal nurse and health assistant, Massimiliano Strappetti, for encouraging him to visit the faithful. "Thank you for bringing me back to the Square,"[37] the pope said. At 5:30 a.m. local time on April 21, the pope's health took a turn for the worse. About an hour later, still in his bed in his apartment, Francis gestured farewell to Strappetti and then slipped into a coma. He was pronounced dead at 7:35 a.m. The search for a new pope would soon begin.

**"Thank you for bringing me back to the Square."[37]**

—Pope Francis

# The First American Pope

When Pope Francis died, the church was divided over his progressive initiatives. For example, in 2023, Francis formally allowed Catholic priests to give same-sex couples a blessing—a radical shift in church policy that pleased progressives but upset traditionalists. The pope also considered the ordination of women as deacons, and opened key positions to them, including membership in the Dicastery for Bishops. His emphasis on synodality, "listening" to the Catholic community as much as leading it, also alienated traditionalists. At the same time, he frustrated progressives by refusing to back down from traditional church teachings on abortion, gay marriage, women's ordination, and priestly celibacy.

## A Referendum

When the papal conclave began, many observers saw the balloting as a referendum on Francis's legacy. Traditionalists hoped the new pope would step back from Francis's progressive reforms. Progressives hoped the new pope would embrace the reforms and further them.

Against this backdrop, various cardinals emerged as possible successors to Francis. These contenders included Cardinal Matteo Zuppi from Italy, a trusted confidante of Francis who would likely continue the late pope's progressive policies. Another highly respected progressive was Cardinal Peter Turkson from Ghana. His choice would signal the importance of the church in Africa, a part of the world where the church's growth is strong. Cardinal Luis Antonio Gokim Tagle from the Philippines is another outspoken progressive. His election would appeal to another part of the world where the church's growth is strong—Asia. Meanwhile, Cardinal Péter Erdő from Hungary would appeal to the traditionalists in the church who were uneasy with Francis's progressive direction. Erdő seemed like an ideal candidate for those who wanted the church to move more in line with the recently sainted Pope John Paul II. There were also two possible compromise candidates. One was Cardinal Pietro Parolin, the Vatican's secretary of state and a skilled diplomat who would be comfortable on the global stage. The other was Robert Prevost.

## Compromise Candidate

Prevost was a proven administrator who had shown that he could handle the demands of running a large organization. Like Zuppi, Prevost shared close ties with Francis, but his moderate recommendations for bishops appealed to traditionalists. At the same time, he had embraced Francis's vision of synodality, ensuring that the church remained a listening institution.

After three rounds of voting, Prevost emerged as the compromise candidate. Although his US citizenship may have concerned those fearful of choosing a pope from a global superpower, his ties to the United States also came with some benefits. Being from the country with the fourth-largest number of Catholics in it—behind only Brazil, Mexico, and the Philippines—Prevost would likely energize the American church, which has been declining in both the number of people who identify as Catholic and in weekly church attendance. His election not only could increase interest in the church, it might also increase financial donations from Catholics in one of the wealthiest countries in the world.

## A Unifying Figure

Since his election, Pope Leo XIV has emerged as the unifying figure that the electors hoped he would be. He has spoken out

*Angela Berners-Wilson, pictured here in 1994, was the first woman to be ordained to the priesthood of the Protestant Church of England. Pope Francis was open to discussions on the ordination of women, but that has not yet been allowed in the Catholic Church.*

on issues of importance to both progressives and traditionalists. In the first months of his papacy, Leo did not push Francis's progressive initiatives any further, but he did not roll them back either. He did, however, show an Augustinian spark of evangelism, calling the faithful to spread the message of the church.

Evangelism was at the heart of his first homily, or sermon, delivered during his first Mass as pope in the Sistine Chapel on May 9, 2025. In it, he described how in the modern world Jesus is commonly "reduced to a kind of charismatic leader or superman,"[38] rather than being seen and worshipped as a divine being. The pope called on members of the church to counteract this loss of faith, which he believes is the root cause of many of today's problems:

> There are many settings in which the Christian faith is considered absurd, meant for the weak and unintelligent. Settings where other securities are preferred, like technology, money, success, power, or pleasure. These are contexts

where it is not easy to preach the Gospel and bear witness to its truth, where believers are mocked, opposed, despised or at best tolerated and pitied. Yet, precisely for this reason, they are the places where our missionary outreach is desperately needed. A lack of faith is often tragically accompanied by the loss of meaning in life, the neglect of mercy, appalling violations of human dignity, the crisis of the family and so many other wounds that afflict our society.[39]

## Calls for Dialogue

Three days later, on May 12, the pope took his message about the challenges of the modern world to members of the news media who were in Rome to cover the papal election. He observed that the current media environment often leaves people lost in a "confusion of loveless languages that are often ideological or

### The Pope Reveals His Personal Aspirations

When Pope Leo XIV addressed ambassadors to the Holy See on May 16, 2025, he revealed a little about himself, including his aspiration to meet people from around the world and why he chose Leo as his papal name:

> Your presence here today is a gift for me. It allows me to renew the Church's aspiration—and my own—to reach out and embrace all individuals and peoples on the Earth, who need and yearn for truth, justice and peace! In a certain sense, my own life experience, which has spanned North America, South America and Europe, has been marked by this aspiration to transcend borders in order to encounter different peoples and cultures. . . .
>
> I chose my name thinking first of all of Leo XIII, the Pope of the first great social Encyclical, *Rerum Novarum* [*Of New Things*]. In this time of epochal change, the Holy See cannot fail to make its voice heard in the face of the many imbalances and injustices that lead, not least, to unworthy working conditions and increasingly fragmented and conflict-ridden societies. Every effort should be made to overcome the global inequalities—between opulence and destitution—that are carving deep divides between continents, countries and even within individual societies.

Pope Leo XIV, "Audience to Members of the Diplomatic Corps Accredited to the Holy See," Holy See, May 16, 2025. www.vatican.va.

Pope Leo at an audience with the press in 2025. The pope talked about the power of the press and urged members of the media to choose their words carefully.

partisan." He urged members of the media to choose their words carefully. "Peace begins with each one of us: in the way we look at others, listen to others and speak about others," he said. "In this sense, the way we communicate is of fundamental importance: we must say 'no' to the war of words and images, we must reject the paradigm of war."[40]

The pope echoed his thoughts about the power of words and the need for peace when he addressed ambassadors to the Holy See on May 16. The pope's words reflected Saint Augustine's teachings about the importance of "interiority," the search for truth through interior reflection. "Peace is built in the heart and from the heart, by eliminating pride and vindictiveness and carefully choosing our words," the pope said. "For words too, not only weapons, can wound and even kill. . . . In this regard, I believe that religions and interreligious dialogue can make a fundamental contribution to fostering a climate of peace."[41]

The next day the pope expanded on his theme of the importance of dialogue in his address to the Centesimus Annus Pro

Pontifice Foundation, a Vatican-based organization established to promote the Catholic Church's social doctrine. The pope first went out of his way to differentiate indoctrination from doctrine. He explained:

> "Indoctrination" is immoral. It stifles critical judgement and undermines the sacred freedom of conscience, even if erroneous. It resists new notions and rejects movement, change or the evolution of ideas in the face of new problems. "Doctrine," on the other hand, as a serious, serene and rigorous discourse, aims to teach us primarily how to approach problems and, even more importantly, how to approach people.[42]

The pope then returned to his theme about the importance of dialogue and listening. He said:

> In the context of the ongoing digital revolution, we must rediscover, emphasize and cultivate our duty to train others in critical thinking, countering temptations to the contrary. . . . There is so little dialogue around us; shouting often replaces it, not infrequently in the form of fake news and irrational arguments proposed by a few loud voices. Deeper reflection and study are essential, as well as a commitment to encounter and listen to the poor, who are a treasure for the Church and for humanity. Their viewpoints, though often disregarded, are vital if we are to see the world through God's eyes.[43]

## Pondering the Rise of Artificial Intelligence

The pope reiterated the importance of critical thinking in light of the emergence of artificial intelligence (AI) in a message to the Second Annual Rome Conference on Artificial Intelligence on May 17, 2025. Drawing on the Augustinian emphasis on "interior truth," the pope emphasized that AI is a tool that derives its "ethical force from the intentions of the individuals that wield" it. He observed that "AI has been used in positive and indeed noble ways to promote greater equality," but he warned that "there is likewise the possibility of its misuse for selfish gain at the expense of others, or worse, to foment conflict and aggression." He called for the church to contribute to an informed and "serene" discussion about the use of AI in light of its impact on human beings. "This entails taking into account the well-being of the human person not only materially, but also intellectually and spiritually; it means safeguarding the inviolable dignity of each human person and respecting the cultural and spiritual riches and diversity of the world's peoples."[44] The pope expressed special concern for the impact of AI on young people:

> **"In the end, authentic wisdom has more to do with recognizing the true meaning of life, than with the availability of data."[45]**
>
> —Pope Leo XIV

> Our youth must be helped, and not hindered, in their journey towards maturity and true responsibility. . . . No generation has ever had such quick access to the amount of information now available through AI. But again, access to data—however extensive—must not be confused with intelligence, which necessarily involves the person's openness to the ultimate questions of life and reflects an orientation toward the True and the Good. In the end, authentic wisdom has more to do with recognizing the true meaning of life, than with the availability of data.[45]

## A Voice for Peace

Leo's first messages applied the church's teachings to important intellectual challenges—AI, the media, and the need for evangelism—but he also spoke out on current events. In his first Sunday noon blessing as pope on May 11, 2025, Leo called for an end to the war between Russia and Ukraine and a ceasefire between Israel and Hamas in the Gaza Strip. "I carry in my heart the sufferings of the beloved Ukrainian people," said the pope. "May everything possible be done to reach an authentic, just and lasting peace, as soon as possible. Let all the prisoners be freed and the children return to their own families." He had similar words for the conflict in Gaza. "I am deeply saddened by what is happening in the Gaza Strip: may there be an immediate ceasefire! Let humanitarian aid be provided to the stricken civil population, and let all the hostages be freed."[46]

The pope did more than speak about peace. He also took action. On May 16, 2025, the pope offered to host direct talks at the Vatican between the leaders of Russia and Ukraine to negotiate a settlement to the three-year war. After his inauguration Mass on May 18, the pope met privately with Ukrainian President Volodymyr Zelenskyy and First Lady Olena Zelenska, who attended the Mass. The leaders discussed the need for peace talks. After the meeting, Zelenskyy posted on X: "For millions of people around the world, the Pontiff is a symbol of hope for peace. The authority and voice of the Holy See can play an important role in bringing

*After his May 18 inauguration Mass, the pope met privately with Ukrainian president Volodymyr Zelenskyy and First Lady Olena Zelenska.*

## A Message to American Youth

On June 14, 2025, thousands of Catholics gathered at Chicago's Rate Field to be a part of Chicago Celebrates Pope Leo XIV, an event hosted by the Archdiocese of Chicago. The pope addressed the crowd via a prerecorded video message.

> To the young people who are gathered here, I'd like to say that you are the promise of hope for so many of us. . . .
>
> Saint Augustine says to us that if we want the world to be a better place, we have to begin with ourselves, we have to begin with our own lives, our own hearts. . . .
>
> We all live with many questions in our hearts. Saint Augustine speaks so often of our "restless" hearts. . . . That restlessness is not a bad thing, and we shouldn't look for ways to put out the fire, to eliminate or even numb ourselves to the tensions that we feel, the difficulties that we experience. We should rather get in touch with our own hearts and recognize that God can work in our lives, through our lives, and through us reach out to other people.

Pope Leo XIV, "Videomessage of the Holy Father Leo XIV to the Young People of Chicago and the Whole World," Holy See, June 14, 2025. www.vatican.va.

this war to an end. We thank the Vatican for its willingness to serve as a platform for direct negotiations between Ukraine and Russia."[47]

On June 4, 2025, Leo called Russian President Vladimir Putin, urging him to negotiate an end to the war. The pope also discussed the humanitarian situation, including the need to allow for the delivery of aid and the exchange of prisoners. According to the Russian government, Putin thanked Leo for offering to help end the war but rejected any peace talks with Ukraine.

Leo continued to speak out for peace when Israel and the United States began a series of air strikes against Iran. In his Sunday address on June 22, 2025, just hours after the United States bombed the sites of three

> **"For millions of people around the world, the Pontiff is a symbol of hope for peace. The authority and voice of the Holy See can play an important role in bringing this war to an end."[47]**
>
> —Volodymyr Zelenskyy, president of Ukraine

nuclear-enrichment facilities in Iran, the pope said the situation in the Middle East was "alarming," and he called for a cessation of hostilities.

> Today more than ever, humanity cries out and calls for peace. This is a cry that requires responsibility and reason, and it must not be drowned out by the din of weapons or the rhetoric that incites conflict. Every member of the international community has a moral responsibility to stop the tragedy of war before it becomes an irreparable chasm. There are no "distant" conflicts when human dignity is at stake.
>
> War does not solve problems; on the contrary, it amplifies them and inflicts deep wounds on the history of peoples, which take generations to heal. No armed victory can compensate for the pain of mothers, the fear of children, or stolen futures.
>
> May diplomacy silence the weapons! May nations chart their futures with works of peace, not with violence and bloodstained conflicts![48]

**"War does not solve problems; on the contrary, it amplifies them and inflicts deep wounds on the history of peoples, which take generations to heal. No armed victory can compensate for the pain of mothers, the fear of children, or stolen futures."[48]**

—Pope Leo XIV

Although Leo did not mention the United States by name, it was clear that the first American pope was more than willing to condemn the actions of the country of his birth. His words were comforting to those who worried that electing a pope from a global superpower might weaken the church, compromising its moral authority. From his statements on war, violence, and technology, it is clear that Leo is guided not by politics or secular philosophy but rather by his church's scriptures and traditions and by his deep personal faith.

# IMPORTANT EVENTS IN THE LIFE OF POPE LEO XIV

## 1955

Robert Francis Prevost is born on September 14 in Chicago, Illinois.

## 1969

Enrolls at St. Augustine Seminary High School in Holland, Michigan.

## 1973

Graduates from high school and enters Villanova University.

## 1977

Graduates with a bachelor's degree in mathematics from Villanova University in June; enters the Order of Saint Augustine as a novice in St. Louis, Missouri, in September.

## 1978

Professes first vows in the Order of Saint Augustine and enrolls at Catholic Theological Union.

## 1981

Professes solemn vows in the Order of Saint Augustine, becoming a friar.

## 1982

Ordained a priest in Rome.

## 1984

Receives licentiate of canon law from the Pontifical University of Saint Thomas Aquinas in Rome.

## 1985

Assigned to first mission in Peru, serving as chancellor of the Territorial Prelature of Chulucanas.

## 1987

Earns doctorate in canon law from the Pontifical University of Saint Thomas Aquinas.

## 1988

Begins service in Trujillo, Peru, as director of formation and seminary rector.

## 1999

Appointed provincial prior of the Augustinian Province of Our Mother of Good Counsel in Chicago.

## 2001

Elected prior general of the Order of Saint Augustine.

## 2014

Consecrated apostolic administrator of Chiclayo, Peru.

## 2015

Concecrated bishop of Chiclayo.

## 2023

Appointed prefect of the Dicastery for Bishops, president of the Pontifical Commission for Latin America, and archbishop.

## 2025

Elevated to cardinal bishop in February; elected pope in May.

# SOURCE NOTES

## Introduction: A New Leader for the Roman Catholic Church

1. Quoted in Vatican News, "Leo XIV Is the New Pope," May 8, 2025. www.vaticannews.va.
2. Quoted in Aryn Baker, "Who Could Be the Next Pope? These Are the Names to Know," *Time*, May 7, 2025. https://partners.time.com.
3. Quoted in Vatican News, "Pope Leo XIV: 'Peace Be with All of You,'" May 8, 2025. www.vaticannews.va.

## Chapter One: Priestly Prodigy

4. Quoted in TOI Lifestyle Desk, "How Pope Leo XIV's Mother and Aunts Shaped His Path to the Papacy," *Times of India* (Mumbai, India), May 9, 2025. https://timesofindia.indiatimes.com.
5. Quoted in Elizabeth Thomas et al., "Pope Leo XIV's Family Tree Shows Black Roots in New Orleans," ABC News, May 9, 2025. https://abcnews.go.com.
6. Quoted in Lauren FitzPatrick, "From Chicago's South Suburbs to Helping Choose the Next Pope," *Chicago Sun-Times*, May 3, 2025. https://chicago.suntimes.com.
7. Quoted in FitzPatrick, "From Chicago's South Suburbs to Helping Choose the Next Pope."
8. Quoted in FitzPatrick, "From Chicago's South Suburbs to Helping Choose the Next Pope."
9. Quoted in FitzPatrick, "From Chicago's South Suburbs to Helping Choose the Next Pope."
10. Quoted in Dorothy Tucker and Todd Feurer, "Pope Leo XIV's Brother Settles Crucial Chicago Debate: Is the Pontiff a White Sox or Cubs Fan?," CBS Chicago, May 8, 2025. www.cbsnews.com.
11. Quoted in Maher Kawash et al., "Dolton Neighbor Told Young Cardinal Robert Prevost He Would Be Pope Someday, New Lenox Brother Says," ABC7 Chicago, May 8, 2025. https://abc7chicago.com.
12. Quoted in Kawash et al., "Dolton Neighbor Told Young Cardinal Robert Prevost He Would Be Pope Someday, New Lenox Brother Says."

13. Quoted in FitzPatrick, "From Chicago's South Suburbs to Helping Choose the Next Pope."
14. Quoted in Kathryn Fink et al., "'Just Overjoyed': Augustinian Priest Reacts to New Pope," NPR, May 8, 2025. www.npr.org.
15. Quoted in Jason Horowitz et al., "Long Drives and Short Homilies: How Father Bob Became Pope Leo," *New York Times*, May 17, 2025. www.nytimes.com.

## Chapter Two: Answering the Call

16. Quoted in Ruth Graham et al., "Pope Leo's Doctoral Dissertation: Thoughts on Power and Authority," *New York Times*, May 22, 2025. www.nytimes.com.
17. Quoted in Mark Zimmermann, "Pope Wants Priests to Be Shepherds Who Encounter Their Flocks," Crux, June 16, 2017. https://cruxnow.com.
18. Quoted in Horowitz et al., "Long Drives and Short Homilies."
19. Quoted in Horowitz et al., "Long Drives and Short Homilies."
20. Quoted in Horowitz et al., "Long Drives and Short Homilies."
21. Quoted in Horowitz et al., "Long Drives and Short Homilies."

## Chapter Three: Rise to Bishop

22. Quoted in Kawash et al., "Dolton Neighbor Told Young Cardinal Robert Prevost He Would Be Pope Someday, New Lenox Brother Says."
23. Pope John Paul II, "Address of John Paul II to the Members of the 180th General Chapter of the Order of St. Augustine (OSA)," Holy See, September 7, 2001. www.vatican.va.
24. Quoted in Horowitz et al., "Long Drives and Short Homilies."
25. Quoted in Horowitz et al., "Long Drives and Short Homilies."
26. Quoted in Walter Sánchez Silva, "Peruvian Bishop Defends Pope Leo XIV Against Accusations of Cover-Up," Catholic News Agency, May 13, 2025. www.catholicnewsagency.com.
27. Quoted in Pablo Ordaz, "Conservatives Accused Prevost of Covering Up Abuse in Peru and the United States Before Conclave," *El País* (Madrid, Spain), May 9, 2025. https://english.elpais.com.
28. Pope John Paul II, "The Ecological Crisis, a Common Responsibility," EWTN, December 8, 1989. www.ewtn.com.
29. Pope Francis, *Encyclical Letter Laudato Si' of the Holy Father Francis on Care for Our Common Home*. Vatican Press, 2015. www.vatican.va.
30. Quoted in Brian Roewe, "Before He Was Pope, Leo XIV Said It's Time for Action on Climate Change," EarthBeat, May 9, 2025. www.ncronline.org.
31. Quoted in Roewe, "Before He Was Pope, Leo XIV Said It's Time for Action on Climate Change."

32. Quoted in Roewe, "Before He Was Pope, Leo XIV Said It's Time for Action on Climate Change."

## Chapter Four: Vatican Leadership

33. Quoted in John Lavenburg, "Pope Taps American to Head Vatican's Powerful Dicastery for Bishops," Crux, January 31, 2023. https://cruxnow.com.
34. Quoted in Horowitz et al., "Long Drives and Short Homilies."
35. Quoted in The Pillar, "Meet the Conclave: Cardinal Robert Francis Prevost," May 2, 2025. www.pillarcatholic.com.
36. Quoted in Vatican News, *February 5 2025 General Audience—Pope Francis*, YouTube, February 5, 2025. https://youtu.be/CYNGkuGTXxs?si=SqGiEi4Z6rgKzCQq.
37. Quoted in Courtney Mares, "The Final Hours of Pope Francis: 'Thank You for Bringing Me Back to the Square,'" Catholic News Agency, April 22, 2025. www.catholicnewsagency.com.

## Chapter Five: The First American Pope

38. Pope Leo XIV, "Full Text of First Public Homily of Pope Leo XIV," OSV News, May 9, 2025. www.ncronline.org.
39. Pope Leo XIV, "Full Text of First Public Homily of Pope Leo XIV."
40. Pope Leo XIV, "Address of the Holy Father Leo XIV to Representatives of the Media," Holy See, May 12, 2025. www.vatican.va.
41. Pope Leo XIV, "Audience to Members of the Diplomatic Corps Accredited to the Holy See," Holy See, May 16, 2025. www.vatican.va.
42. Pope Leo XIV, "Address of His Holiness Pope Leo XIV to Members of the 'Centesimus Annus Pro Pontifice' Foundation," Holy See, May 17, 2025. www.vatican.va.
43. Pope Leo XIV, "Address of His Holiness Pope Leo XIV to Members of the 'Centesimus Annus Pro Pontifice' Foundation."
44. Pope Leo XIV, "Message of Pope Leo XIV to Participants in the Second Annual Conference on Artificial Intelligence, Ethics, and Corporate Governance," Holy See, May 17, 2025. www.vatican.va.
45. Pope Leo XIV, "Message of Pope Leo XIV to Participants in the Second Annual Conference on Artificial Intelligence, Ethics, and Corporate Governance."
46. Pope Leo XIV, "Regina Caeli, Loggia of the Blessings of St. Peter's Basilica," Holy See, May 11, 2025. www.vatican.va.
47. Volodymyr Zelenskyy (@ZelenskyyUa), "After the inauguration Mass, we had a meeting with Pope Leo XIV," X, May 18, 2025. https://twitter.com/ZelenskyyUa/status/1924099530510721138.
48. Pope Leo XIV, "Most Holy Body and Blood of Christ," Holy See, June 22, 2025. www.vatican.va.

# FOR FURTHER RESEARCH

## Books

Matthew Bunson, *Leo XIV: Portrait of the First American Pope*. EWTN, 2025.

Jesús Colina, *Pope Leo XIV*. Our Sunday Visitor, 2025.

Editors of *Life*, *Pope Leo XIV*. Dotdash Meredith, 2025.

Mike Schmitz et al., *When the White Smoke Clears*. Ascension, 2025.

Christopher White, *Pope Leo XIV: Inside the Conclave and the Dawn of a New Papacy*. Loyola, 2025.

## Internet Sources

Lauren FitzPatrick, "From Chicago's South Suburbs to Helping Choose the Next Pope," *Chicago Sun-Times*, May 3, 2025. https://chicago.suntimes.com.

Pope Francis, *Encyclical Letter Laudato Si' of the Holy Father Francis on Care for Our Common Home*. Vatican Press, 2015. www.vatican.va.

Ruth Graham et al., "Pope Leo's Doctoral Dissertation: Thoughts on Power and Authority," *New York Times*, May 22, 2025. www.nytimes.com.

Jason Horowitz et al., "Long Drives and Short Homilies: How Father Bob Became Pope Leo," *New York Times*, May 17, 2025. www.nytimes.com.

Pope Leo XIV, "Message of Pope Leo XIV to Participants in the Second Annual Conference on Artificial Intelligence, Ethics, and Corporate Governance," Holy See, May 17, 2025. www.vatican.va.

## Websites

**Catholic News Agency**
www.catholicnewsagency.com
The Catholic News Agency is a global news service providing news about the Catholic Church, the Holy See, and the pope.

**Holy See**
www.vatican.va
The official website of the Holy See is a resource for information about the Vatican and the pope, including text of the pope's speeches, audiences, homilies, letters, and messages.

**Order of Saint Augustine**
www.augustinianorder.org
The official website of the Order of Saint Augustine includes information about the order's news, history, beliefs, and leaders.

**Vatican News**
www.vaticannews.va
Vatican News is the news portal of the Holy See. It includes news about the pope, the Vatican, the Catholic Church, and the world.

# INDEX

*Note: Boldface page numbers indicate illustrations.*

# PICTURE CREDITS

Cover: Marco Iacobucci Epp/Shutterstock

6: Marco Iacobuccci Epp/Shutterstock
9: ARCHIVIO GBB/Alamy Stock Photo
12: Maria Grazia Piccciarella/Alamy Stock Photo
15: ARCHIVIO GBB/Alamy Stock Photo
18: ARCHIVIO GBB/Alamy Stock Photo
20: Independent Photo Agency Srl/Alamy Stock Photo
23: Abaca Press/Alamy Stock Photo
28: AGENZIA SINTESI/Alamy Stock Photo
31: Christian Vinces/Shutterstock
33: Godong/Shutterstock
36: Independent Photo Agency Srl/Alamy Stock Photo
39: Abaca Press/Alamy Stock Photo
41: Marco Iacobucci Epp/Shutterstock
45: PA Images/Alamy Stock Photo
47: Alessia Pierdomenico/Shutterstock
50: Independent Photo Agency Srl/Alamy Stock Photo

# ABOUT THE AUTHOR

Bradley Steffens is a novelist, a poet, and an award-winning author of more than seventy nonfiction books for children and young adults.